YOUR PERFECT *partner* WON'T BE PERFECT

A TRUTHFUL DATING GUIDE

SIMA TAPARIA

Sourcebooks

Contents

CHAPTER 3: Flexibility is everything.

CHAPTER 4: Utilize your resources.

CHAPTER 5: The relationship won't work unless you do.

CHAPTER 6: Stay positive. It will all work out.

Introduction

In India, there are two types of marriages. A *love marriage* occurs when two people find each other—often by happenstance—and make the decision to move forward in a relationship together. It's what most Americans think of when they think of marriage. It's the boy-meets-girl relationship you see in American film and television, where a meet-cute is followed by love and commitment and families aren't even introduced until things start to get "serious."

The other type of marriage is simply that… *marriage*. Western countries may refer to these as "arranged marriages," but that's not what we call them in India. To us, an arranged marriage is the norm. It's a long-standing tradition that acknowledges the importance of family in relationships. In this marriage, it's not just two people entering a union, it's two families.

This concept of marriage may seem strange to an American audience, but when you think about it, it makes sense. Think of everything that's at stake for a parent when their child marries—finances, reputations, family dynamics, lifestyles, community, and more. To us, marriage is bigger than two people making the commitment to love each other forever. It's a commitment between two families to become one. To create a bigger, better life for the next generation. It's only logical that these two families should play an active role in the process, right?

This may not sound romantic—it's rarely the story of fairy tales and rom-coms—but in my experience, it works. It worked for the clients I've matched, it worked for my ancestors who practiced it for centuries, and it worked for me.

In 1983, my father's sister was at a wedding, where she met Anup, a young man born to a wonderful family with strong business relations. She quickly shared this news with my father, and he arranged for our two families to meet. If Anup and I had met organically, the "love marriage" way, who knows what would have happened? Who knows if we would have gotten married at all? But with the guidance of our parents and the wisdom of our families, a union was formed. More than forty years later, Anup and I are still married, living a beautiful life together.

This is what I've always wanted for myself, but it's also been my lifelong dream to help others find this kind of joy. In fact, one of my happiest memories is the first successful match I ever made for two clients. And the memory is so much greater than the fact that I helped two people, it's that I got to help two whole *families*. (Can you imagine that kind of fulfillment? With every match, I'm able to benefit dozens of people—parents, aunts, uncles, siblings, you name it!) So to me, marriage is so much more than romantic love and chemistry. To me, marriage is how we set the course for the future.

How to Use This Book

Many of you reading this book may be thinking to yourselves, "That all sounds great, but we don't really do arranged marriages where I come from, so this wouldn't work for me." And you may be right; you might live in a community where this practice isn't common, so the guidance and resources aren't in place for you to pursue this kind of marriage. And that's fine! You may not be able to do things exactly as we do them in India, but that doesn't mean the long-practiced, tried-and-true wisdom from Indian matchmaking can't help you too.

What I hope for you, reader, is that you can build a better understanding of how Indian marriages work and learn to incorporate some of this wisdom into your own life. If you're single and looking for a life partner, let this book serve as a guide. Let it inform your understanding of marriage as an institution, let it help you frame the philosophy of how you view marriage, and let it guide you in the right direction to choosing a better future.

If you're a parent, sibling, family member, or friend reading this thinking, "I wish so-and-so could find their perfect match already," then this book can help you too! Like I said before, marriage isn't just about two people—it's about two families. You can use the wisdom in this book to help you become a better guide to your single family members and friends. Successful marriages are built within their communities—let this book help you become a contributing member in that community!

At the end of the day, we all want the same things in life, regardless of where we're from. We all want to live happy lives, and we all want to share our lives with people we love. No matter what motivated you to pick up this book, know that the end goal is the same for all of us, and let this wisdom guide you to a better, happier life with more love and hope than ever before.

CHAPTER

1

BEING PICKY IS OVERRATED.

Setting Your Standards

This is easily one of the biggest issues I face when working with clients: Everyone has their dream partner completely detailed in their mind. They'll say to me, "Sima, I need a man who's smart, ambitious, funny, well-read, well-traveled, sensitive, passionate, responsible, good at sports, not allergic to dogs, a good cook, handsome, energetic, outgoing, clean, well-organized, emotionally mature, creative, and interesting... Oh, and he needs to be more than six feet tall." No wonder you're having a hard time finding that guy—even Prince Charming himself doesn't meet this description! Yet so many people wait and wait for that guy to come along, so it's inevitable that they'll be disappointed when he never does.

I know I used a woman's "dream guy" as the example in the opening paragraph, but don't think I'm only talking to women right now. Men are just as guilty. Their demands for a partner are just as high, and they need this dose of reality too.

Here's the thing: Most single people think a relationship would be impossible with anyone other than the (fictional) ideal mate they've concocted in their heads, but that's rooted in fantasy, not reality. In reality, people are nuanced and the world is messy. Nobody (and I mean *nobody*) will fit the entire checklist in your head. But that doesn't mean your perfect match isn't out there. It means they're waiting for you to drop a few of those standards so they have room to be human and grow *with you* in a relationship.

———

In this section, the wisdom I share will help you understand which qualities are important to prioritize and which unrealistic standards are holding you back from a truly great future.

1

The materialistic things aren't
important and won't determine if
you'll have a happy life together.

Look at the person, not what they own
or the shallow things that might "define"
them. Jobs, cars, houses, money—these
are temporary things that a person
owns, not a lasting part of who they are.

The material things in life will change,
so don't count on those things
to make a relationship happy.

2

Finding a partner is not like
ordering from a menu.

You don't get to pick and choose all the
toppings you want, and certainly will
never see *all* the ingredients up front.

3

Compromise is important in every stage of a relationship, but that's especially true at the beginning.

In case it isn't clear at this point in the book yet, *nobody is perfect*, so nobody is going to meet the standard of perfection in your head.

Start the practice of compromise early and you'll be poised for a healthier future.

4

Learn to separate the things you *want* in a partner from the things you *need* in a partner.

A partner who's funny or well-traveled may be something you want, but does a person's ability to crack a good joke or their knowledge of tourist destinations really mean they'll be a good spouse to you?

5

The higher the standards, the more difficult the search. If you've been at this for a while, take a step back and ask yourself, "Are the people I'm meeting really not that great? Or are my standards just way too high?"

You'll be amazed how many people who don't check *all* your boxes are actually great catches!

6

Be honest: If the roles were reversed, would you meet your own criteria for a partner?

Be gracious and treat others how you want to be treated.

7

Being picky is overrated!

Some people pride themselves on being picky, thinking that their selectiveness gives them a more elite status. But in my experience, being picky doesn't impress anyone; it just makes your life harder.

So don't be afraid to try new things. You might even learn that you like them.

8

Hobbies don't determine compatibility.

Stop trying to find someone who likes all
the same things as you and understand
that *similarity* and *compatibility*
are two very different things.

9

On that note, variety is the spice of life!

Learn to appreciate how exciting
it can be to find a partner with
different tastes and interests.

10

You don't have to sacrifice your values to create realistic standards.

Start with the values that are most important to you (family, honesty, loyalty, etc.) and let these be the foundation of your connection. If someone can't connect with your core principles, that could be a real problem. If someone just doesn't share all the same opinions, though? That's not such a big deal.

Opinions will change; values rarely do.

CHAPTER

2

DON'T CROWD THE POOL!

Plenty of Fish in the Sea

Another common mistake I encounter when helping clients is a mentality of "more is better." People want to see all of their options, they want to make informed decisions, and they want to experience everything before they make a choice. This is fine if you're test-driving cars or shopping for new jeans, but with a life partner, it's a little tricky. People are more complex than cars or clothing, so there's a lot more to weigh when thinking about which one is the best fit for you.

When working with clients, I'll often show them only one or two options at a time. I'll present the client with a sheet of paper that contains another person's biodata—all the little facts and bits of data you could use to describe them—and ask what they think. If it's a no, we move on to a different option. If it's a yes, we stay focused on that person for the time being.

We know there are plenty of fish in the sea, and everyone wants to see *all* of them before they make a selection. But let me warn you: A crowded dating pool is impossible to move around in. Adding too many options to the mix only confuses people, and it guarantees you'll stay focused on the shallow little things that don't matter. You can't get to know all of these people deeply when your time and attention is divided among them. Take your time, focus on what's in front of you, and don't overwhelm yourself unnecessarily.

———

In this section, you'll learn how to focus on what matters and date smarter, not harder.

11

Have you ever been to a restaurant with a gigantic menu, full of meals that appeal to you in different ways? After you order, are you ever satisfied with your selection when there are so many other options that still have your eye? The same thing can be asked about dating.

Do you ever really enjoy the time you spend with someone if you're thinking about the other people sitting in your inbox?

Quit thinking about all the other things that might be out there, and focus on what's in front of you now.

12

Pictures aren't everything.

So many people spend their time mindlessly swiping left and right on pictures in dating apps, making quick judgments on looks alone.

And at the end of it, what do you have? A pool of people who are physically attractive but are probably horrible matches for you.

Don't spend your time judging photos. You need to meet people to know if you like them or not.

13

How many books can you read at once, really? If you have ten books open on a table, are you able to absorb all their information, or are you confusingly jumping from page to page, forgetting what you just read?

This is what it's like trying to assess too many people at once. I've said it before, and I'll say it again: People are complex.

If you have too many people in front of you at once, you're bound to be confused—and confused people don't make good choices.

14

The more options you have, the more things you have to weigh against each other. "Brad is tall and handsome, but his teeth aren't straight. Jake is ambitious and successful, but his table manners are lacking. Luke is sweet and charming, but he isn't an intellectual."

How are you supposed to weigh all these different qualities in all their different combinations against each other, really? It's a recipe for confusion and indecision, and it's more work than you need to put yourself through.

15

Every match, every date, every person you consider is a potential life partner.

You need to take them all seriously.

16

In my line of business, when a meeting between two clients is successful, things move fast. But that wouldn't be possible if both those clients were insistent on "keeping their options open."

You need to be ready for things to move forward when the right match happens.

17

Think about things from the reverse perspective: do you want the people you're seeing to have other potential partners on their mind while they're with you?

Give each match the attention you want in return.

18

Practice mindfulness.

Meditation is beneficial in every aspect of life, and that's true of your romantic life as well. Meditate on how you feel about a person, and stay grounded in the present moment. Your mind will want to rush to all the future possibilities and all the things that could go wrong, but time spent worrying about things that haven't happened is time wasted.

Stay in the moment and be mindful.

19

Trust the process.

If you get to know someone
and don't think they're the right
person for you, that's okay.

Don't be discouraged and don't
think you need a wider net; just know
that it's time to move forward.

20

Know that nobody will be
perfect at the first meeting.

Connection takes time, so stay focused.

Distractions will only guarantee that
the connection never happens.

CHAPTER

3

FLEXIBILITY IS EVERYTHING.

An Open Mind and an Open Heart

I was standing at the baggage claim of an airport when I met a nice family—a lovely couple with a daughter. After exchanging pleasantries, we fell into a deeper conversation, and I got to know the dynamics of their family, their values, and that their daughter was in need of a soulmate. I already had someone in mind whose family would blend well with theirs, so right there in the airport, I made a match.

It wasn't something that was planned, and

this family certainly didn't walk up to baggage claim expecting to walk away with a new son-in-law. But they were open-minded, and they were happy to embrace opportunities. And it paid off for them! These things happen at odd places and at odd times. But they won't happen for you if you aren't open to them.

———

In this section, you'll learn the importance of flexibility and an open mindset when it comes to marriage.

21

You're never going to find your perfect match if you aren't even willing to meet them and try. It's as simple as that.

22

Be open to the concept of destiny.

You have no idea when new people
will pop into your life, and you have
no idea when one of those people
will be your future spouse.

Be open to the possibility that some
things are determined by a higher
power, and your responsibility is
to welcome the opportunity.

23

Be open-minded about the qualities of your partner.

This goes back to Section 1, but it bears repeating in this section as well.

You need to be open to people who might not meet the predetermined expectations in your head.

24

An open mind creates
flexibility—a quality that no
marriage can survive without.

Life is going to bring you constant
changes and uncertainty, your ability to
be flexible determines how you'll adapt
and thrive under new circumstances.

25

There will always be a downside to everything, and there will always be a reason to not do something.

Even when faced with the ideal mate, people ask themselves, "Is this too good to be true?"

Nothing will ever be entirely positive or free of risk, so it's up to you to make the best of each situation and be open to the possibilities.

26

We spend so much time in life worrying about the future, worrying if we're making the right choices, worrying about what comes next, worrying, worrying, worrying. Only closed minds let the worrying stop them from experiencing life.

If you have an open mind, you may see the potential for harm or know the possible outcomes, but you won't dwell on them. You'll be informed of what could go wrong, but you'll live a life pursuing all the things that could go right.

27

Nothing will ever happen unless
you embrace the moment.

Be an active player in finding your
person—don't just wait on the sidelines.

28

Don't just be open-minded about people, be open-minded about situations too.

Things may not seem perfect on paper. Whether it's entering a long-distance relationship or going to an amusement park on a first date when you truly hate roller coasters.

You'll never know what's possible if you don't try.

29

Be open to the wisdom of others.

If you're reading this book, then
hopefully you already are, but
don't be afraid to seek advice
and hear new perspectives.

30

Openness isn't just a willingness to act—it's a mindset.

It isn't about entering new situations with pessimism or cynicism. It's about entering them with no preconceived notions, completely free of judgment.

Practice this mindset, and the positive results will follow.

CHAPTER

4

UTILIZE YOUR RESOURCES.

Marriage Is a Family Affair

In India, marriage is so much more than romantic love. Marriage is the melding of families, communities, traditions, and values. Marriage affects more than the two people inside of it; it sets the path for two families moving forward into the future.

It's an institution that promises life and growth. It's the growth of a family and the growth of a community as long-held rituals, beliefs, and ways of life are passed down to the next generation.

With all these stakeholders, you're guaranteed to have people in your corner who want to see you succeed and want to see you have a healthy marriage and a happy life. These are the people who can help guide you toward the partnership you want.

———

In this section, you'll understand all the resources available to you and learn to lean on them for support and guidance.

31

Don't go through the dating world alone!

Your parents have wisdom to share,
and their role is going to be important
as your family joins with another.

Seek their advice, and let them help
you make the process easier.

32

So many couples over prioritize privacy in their relationships. So when difficulties arise, they keep to themselves and struggle with the issues alone.

But why would you struggle alone when so many other people are here to help you?

Marriage doesn't work without the guidance and support of parents, so be open and honest with them.

33

Your friends and the community
around you are also important
for your success in life.

Don't let your pride get in the way of
making the most of that community.

They have connections, and
one of those connections might
be your perfect match!

34

Seek out specialists who can help you.

For example, I often go to a face reader—a person with a unique ability to understand people's characters, personalities, and destinies through their physical appearances—to seek guidance on matching my clients successfully.

Keep practicing an open mindset, and don't be afraid to step out of your comfort zone to ask for new guidance.

35

Pay attention to horoscopes.

Horoscopes are like insurance for
a happy marriage and can help you
understand whether or not you're
compatible with someone.

36

Palmistry—also known as palm reading—
has deep roots in Indian culture.

This is the art of studying a person's
physical markings and the lines
of their hands to illuminate their
character and their future.

Many people I work with turn to palm
readers to better understand their
compatibility with a potential partner.

37

Tarot readers also play a role in how we approach marriage in India.

All of these ancient practices—tarot, palmistry, horoscopes—have bled into American culture and are available for you to use.

Why not try them?

38

Lean on your own family, but also seek the guidance of your potential partner's family.

If things work out, they'll be your family too one day, so seek their advice and involvement early on.

39

Look to other married couples in
your community and in your family.

Seek their wisdom and listen
to what they say.

40

And, of course, consider working
with a matchmaker!

Matchmakers are great resources for
bringing people together and forming
happy unions between families.

CHAPTER

5

THE RELATIONSHIP WON'T WORK UNLESS YOU DO.

Hard Work
Pays Off

Often, people are picky about their partners right off the bat because they're too near-sighted to see how much time, work, and effort goes into a truly good relationship. They don't realize that life is about growth and change, so they want everything to be perfect from the very beginning. But that's just not realistic for a healthy marriage.

If you rely on your families to advise you into a good relationship, you can start the marriage on a solid foundation and build from there. Romantic love and physical attraction are great things to have, but they can fizzle over time. Companionship, however, continues to build. As you go through life and face new and greater challenges, you're going to want a true companion by your side. And that companionship something you gain through hard, persistent work.

_____

In this section, you'll learn that relationships aren't always easy and that the strongest ones take effort.

41

I've emphasized the importance of compromising when it comes to standards and expectations while searching for a partner, but I also need to mention how important it is once the relationship begins.

No matter how strong the match, there will always be obstacles that get in the way and new challenges that arise.

The only way you'll make it past those obstacles is through compromise.

42

Long-distance relationships get
a bad rap. Are they hard? Yes.
But aren't all relationships hard,
regardless of location? Also yes.

If the connection is right, the
distance is just another challenge
to work through together.

Long-distance relationships are normal,
and with a little work, entirely possible.

43

Your spouse is a lifelong companion.

Building the trust required for true companionship takes time and effort, but boy is it worth it.

Through that work, you have someone you can confide in, process emotions with, and gain strength from.

44

Some people have asked me how a person should know when they've met "the one."

The truth is, you'll never really *know*. When you feel a spark or a strong romantic pull, it may feel like that sense of "knowing," but even relationships that start with a strong spark can end with a sad fizzle.

The only way to truly know you're in the right relationship is to watch it over time, to see how committed you both are to adjusting, compromising, being patient, and being flexible. Those are the things that make a marriage last.

45

It can take a long time for a couple to get together and only a moment for them to separate.

The hard work doesn't end after "I Do."

46

One of the hardest practices to master is communication.

Work hard on this skill and communicate openly with your partner and with your family.

47

Don't look at other couples and assume their lives are perfect or that there's something wrong with you for not having that type of relationship.

No relationship is perfect, and no relationship is without work.

If you know a happy couple that you look up to, ask them about the work they put into it. They'll have plenty of wisdom to share, and it won't be, "It's just easy! We don't work on anything!"

48

As much as you need to be willing to work on the relationship, you need to be willing to work on yourself too.

The ability to grow together still requires that you can grow at all.

49

Nothing that starts in "perfect" conditions stays that way, so don't strive for perfection before the relationship even begins.

Start with the foundations of family and values, then work on building a connection from there.

50

And don't forget that the hard
work isn't yours alone to bear.

A successful marriage requires work
from both partners and from their
families who guide and support them.

6

STAY POSITIVE.
IT WILL ALL
WORK OUT.

It Will Happen

Relationships may be hard work, but they're not something to look at with pessimism or dread. The work that goes into finding a match and building a life together isn't easy, but it's rewarding in ways you can't even imagine.

If you're searching for a partner now, know that this is a journey. Rarely do people just bump into their future spouse, immediately hit it off, and then live happily ever after. In Indian marriages, there's a whole community of people helping two families come together, and from there, the hard work is put in to ensure a long, happy marriage. So don't be discouraged in moments when the match doesn't work. Just know that destiny will intervene when the time is right, and it will happen for you eventually.

—

In this section, enjoy some final bits of wisdom to encourage you in the pursuit of marriage.

51

Destiny is real. It guides us along
and brings us the opportunities
we were meant to have.

It's up to you whether or not you
take those opportunities.

52

This may be cliché, but it's true:
If it's meant to be, it will be.

53

Nothing will happen until
you're ready for it.

Do the work to get ready, and
great things will come.

54

You get out of life what you put into it.

If you open your mind and put
positivity into the world, the world
will return that positivity to you.

A Note to the Reader

Thank you for taking the time to open your mind to ideas that may be new to you. Matchmaking is a long-standing tradition in India, based on centuries of wisdom. I know you may not exist in a culture where matchmaking is common, but in my culture, it has been a successful and beloved practice. Hopefully, some of the wisdom from this ancient art can inspire you today in a modern dating landscape.

About the Author

Sima Taparia has been a matchmaker since 2005 and resides in Mumbai. She hails from the famous industrial family of Lahoti of Kalaburagi (Gulbarga, Karnataka), and in 1983 she married into the Taparia family, an industrial family in Mumbai. She has always been fond of networking and meeting people, and she is associated with many clubs and social organizations. With more than two decades of experience in the field, Sima Taparia has earned her reputation as a respected and trusted matchmaker. Her expertise lies in understanding her clients' preferences, cultural backgrounds, and personal values, enabling her to make a compatible match.

Her documentary *A Suitable Girl* won an award at the Tribeca Film festival in 2017, and Sima stars on Netflix's Emmy-nominated hit reality show *Indian Matchmaking*, which portrays the Indian values that have been an important part of her culture for thousands of years. She is also featured on Netflix's *Fabulous Lives of Bollywood Wives*, *Mika Di Voti*, and *Bigg Boss*.

Sima was presented with the Bharat Gaurav award by HRH Sheikh Mohmmad of Dubai for displaying Indian values to the world and was honored by the Governor of Maharashtra for empowering women. She also received the Trendsetter Award in Mumbai and the Elite Influential Indian Award in New York.

With her warm demeanor and insightful guidance, Sima Taparia continues to assist individuals and families in their quest for meaningful and compatible relationships. Her dedication to her clients' happiness and her deep understating of cultural nuances have made her a sought-after matchmaker in the world of arranged marriages.

Published by Sourcebooks
1935 Brookdale RD, Naperville, IL 60563-2773
(630) 961-3900
sourcebooks.com

Cataloging-in-Publication Data is on file with the Library of Congress.

Printed and bound in the United States of America.
MA 10 9 8 7 6 5 4 3 2 1